Gordon Gre... ...ol
...IL 60564

W9-AUJ-926

30018000321?0K

# CHOPIN'S WORLD

ANN MALASPINA

Gordon Gregory Middle School
2621 Springdale Circle
Naperville, IL 60564

rosen publishing's
rosen central®

New York

*To my husband, Robert Harold, who plays all kinds of music*

Published in 2008 by The Rosen Publishing Group, Inc.
29 East 21st Street, New York, NY 10010

Copyright © 2008 by The Rosen Publishing Group, Inc.

First Edition

All rights reserved. No part of this book may be reproduced in any form without permission in writing from the publisher, except by a reviewer.

**Library of Congress Cataloging-in-Publication Data**

Malaspina, Ann (1957– ).
Chopin's world/Ann Malaspina.—1st ed.
     p. cm.—(Music throughout history)
Includes bibliographical references (p.   ) and index.
ISBN-13: 978-1-4042-0723-3
ISBN-10: 1-4042-0723-6 (library binding)
1. Chopin, Frédéric, 1810–1849—Juvenile literature.
2. Composers—Biography—Juvenile literature. I. Title.
ML3930.C46M16 2006
786.2092—dc22
[B]
                                        2005031281

*Manufactured in the United States of America*

**On the cover:** The composer Frédéric Chopin (1810–1849), born near Warsaw, Poland, became best known for his creative and expressive piano melodies and piano concerti.

# CONTENTS

An artist depicted composer Frédéric Chopin, the Polish Poet of the Piano, as a young man in this painting.

# INTRODUCTION

On October 11, 1830, a pale, slender young man named Frédéric Chopin leaned over the pianoforte on the stage of the National Theater in Warsaw. The wealthiest citizens of the Polish capital, and the pianist's friends and family, filled the concert hall. They were eager to hear Chopin's latest music. The conductor, Carlo Soliva, raised his baton, and the violinists lifted their bows. The Piano Concerto no. 1 in E Minor opened with the fast Allegro movement. The strings, woodwinds, and brass began, as the audience waited in anticipation for the piano. Then Chopin struck his first notes. His light touch and soaring melodies, both delicate and bold, took the audience's breath away. No one had ever heard such harmonies, or witnessed such perfect technique.

At the time, Chopin was just twenty years old, but he was known in Warsaw as a master of the pianoforte, or piano, and a promising composer. He finished writing the concerto only months earlier. The Allegro movement was followed by a slower Adagio. Dreamy and passionate, the Adagio had a haunting piano solo. Woven into the final rondo movement, was a lively mazurka, the favorite Polish folk dance.

As the notes faded, the audience applauded loudly. Chopin stood and bowed, again and again. The reviews for the performance and the composition were ecstatic. Chopin's concerto was immediately declared a work of genius. Pleased, Chopin sent a letter to a close friend the following day. He wrote, "Yesterday's concert was a success; I haste to let you know. I inform your Lordship that I was not a bit, not a bit nervous, and played the way I play when I'm alone, and it went well . . . No one hissed, and I had to bow four times."

A dazzling career lay ahead for Chopin, but not in his native Poland. He needed more freedom to create his music. Weeks later, he left Poland, never to return. Chopin had great things to accomplish in a life that would be cut short by illness. Physically weak but with a zest for living, Chopin created a new language for the piano. His music was personal and expressive. Yet beneath his startling harmonies, Chopin could be dark and disturbing. "Chopin's works are cannons concealed among flowers," said the composer Robert Schumann, according to biographer Tad Szulc. The world came to adore the so-called poet of the piano, whose music made people sing and cry.

Although he never returned home, Poland would not forget the composer who transformed the folk songs of peasants into concert music. When the Germans invaded Warsaw in 1944 during World War II (1939–1945), Nazi soldiers knocked over the statue of Chopin in Lazienki Park, and melted it down for ammunition. The Nazis forbade the Poles from playing the songs of their favorite composer, for they knew Chopin represented Poland's spirit then as he still does today.

# CHAPTER ONE

## Child of Poland

Chopin's story began with an adventurous father. The Frenchman Nicolas Chopin, like his son, was a restless child in a small village in Lorraine. His father owned vineyards, but Nicolas did not want to become a winemaker. Instead, he wanted to see the world. When Nicolas was sixteen, he moved to Poland and found a job as a bookkeeper in Warsaw. In 1794, he volunteered for the Warsaw National Guard to defend Poland against Russia. Though he was short and slight, like his son would be, he became a captain. As Nicolas Chopin grew fond of his adopted country, he changed his name to Mikolaj, Polish for Nicolas.

In 1802, Mikolaj took a job as a tutor for the wealthy Skarbek family in Zelazowa Wola, a small village about thirty-seven miles (sixty kilometers) west of Warsaw.

The village of Zelazowa Wola, Poland, where Chopin was born in 1810, lies outside Warsaw. Today the manor of Chopin's birthplace is a museum and is open to the public.

Mikolaj was a natural teacher. He loved reading and knew many languages. He also played the violin and flute. Mikolaj fell in love with Tekla Justyna Krzyzanowska, who was known as Justyna. The daughter of a Polish farmer, Justyna was related to the Skarbek family and cared for their children. Like Mikolaj, Justyna was musical; she had a beautiful soprano singing voice and played the piano. The couple married in a small Catholic church in the medieval village of Brochow in 1806, and moved into a house on the estate. They soon had a daughter whom they named Ludwika.

Three years later, on March 1, 1810, Justyna gave birth to the couple's only son, though the official birth records marked the date as February 22. Mikolaj and Justyna named their son Fryderyk, after the Skarbek's son, and

Francisczek, after Mikolaj's father. The baby was christened Fryderyk Franciszek Szopen in St. Roch's Church in Brochow on April 23. ("Szopen" is the Polish spelling of "Chopin.") Later, Chopin used the French spelling, Frédéric François Chopin.

With a growing family to support, Mikolaj needed a lucrative job. Less than a year after Frédéric's birth, the family moved to Warsaw, the capital of Poland. Mikolaj was hired to teach French at the Warsaw Lyceum, or high school. The family moved into a wing of the old palace that housed the school. Before long, Frédéric had two younger sisters, Justyna and Emilia.

The Chopin family was very close. As the only boy, Frédéric got plenty of attention. He loved to play tricks, mimic people, and tease his sisters. A talented artist, he kept a notebook of sketches. He and his sisters performed plays. One summer, Frédéric and Emilia even wrote their own newspaper. Though they were never wealthy, the Chopins led a comfortable life. They had many bourgeois, or middle-class, friends, such as doctors, professors, and musicians, and their home was filled with lively conversation, music, and laughter.

The Chopin family enjoyed life in the city. It was a good time to live in Warsaw. After decades of war, the city was calm. At night, operas, ballets, and orchestras filled Warsaw's National Theater. As he grew up, Frédéric often attended shows, including Italian operas, which inspired him for a lifetime.

## LEARNING TO PLAY

Frédéric was very young when he first heard his mother and sister Ludwika play the piano. Although no one

## A Nation Under Siege

By the time Chopin was born in 1810, Poland was a nation divided and conquered. The large country in central Europe, bordering the Baltic Sea, had a strong identity. Yet Poland had become a battlefield in a power struggle between European nations. The Polish people proved no match for constantly invading armies.

It wasn't always like that. In the 1500s, Poland was a thriving empire that stretched across eastern and central Europe. But over the next 200 years, Poland fell to stronger powers. In 1772, Austria, Prussia, and Russia divided Poland into three parts. Unable to win back independence, Poland was partitioned in 1793 and 1795.

Hoping to take back their nation, Polish men joined the army of Napoléon Bonaparte, the French emperor bent on conquering Europe. Napoléon won Poland in 1807, and he called it the Grand Duchy of Warsaw. A Polish government was established. After Napoléon was defeated, Poland was again ruled by Austria, Prussia, and Russia. The small Kingdom of Poland was formed in Warsaw, but the Poles were still under the thumb of the Russian czar. After the Russians crushed the Polish Uprising of 1830, life for the Poles worsened.

Poland did not regain independence until after World War I (1914–1918). But the twentieth century proved no less difficult for Poles. Germany and the Soviet Union invaded Poland during World War II. More than 6 million Poles died during the war, including 3 million Polish Jews. The Germans deported another 2.5 million Poles for forced labor. The Warsaw beloved by Chopin was bombed and burned. After the war, the Soviet Union held eastern Poland and installed a Communist government there. Finally, in 1989, free democratic elections were held in Poland, thanks to Solidarity, the organization of free trade unions that pushed fearlessly for democracy and freedom.

showed him how to find the keys or count the beats, Frédéric was soon playing alone. By the time their son was six years old, the Chopins found him a teacher, Wojciech Zywny, an elderly violinist and pianist from Bohemia. Zywny saw that Frédéric had talent. Frédéric sped through his lessons and quickly mastered difficult compositions. Zywny made sure he played pieces by his favorite composers, Bach and Mozart. Frédéric practiced Bach each day. He learned the balance and harmony of the baroque music of the eighteenth century.

Within a short time, Frédéric became devoted to the piano. One legend says he slept with wine corks between his fingers so his small hands could develop a wider reach over the keys. He also liked to improvise, or create original music. He was just seven years old when he wrote two traditional Polish court dances known as polonaises. Mikolaj wrote his son's music on paper, and before long, a Warsaw printer published Chopin's first composition, the Polonaise in G Minor. According to Szulc, a reviewer declared the boy "a true musical genius." Frédéric felt he was a natural composer. When he was eight years old, he sent a note to his father on the holiday of Saint Nicholas that read: "Dear Papa! I could express my feelings more easily if they could be put into notes of music . . ."

Frédéric first performed in public in 1818 at a charity concert. He played a piano concerto by Adalbert Gyrowetz, a popular Czech composer. Frédéric didn't realize he created a stir. One story says he told his mother after the concert that everyone was admiring the fine white collar of his shirt. He didn't realize that people were calling him a child prodigy, like they had Wolfgang Amadeus Mozart (1756–1791), the composer from Austria. Soon, he was invited to perform in the homes of Warsaw's leading citizens. At these salons, or gatherings, Frédéric gained confidence. He learned to dress like a gentleman and developed fine manners. Throughout his life, Frédéric sought this world of privilege, but he never became wealthy.

One of Chopin's earliest compositions, written when he was eight, is the Polonaise, a traditional Polish court dance. Chopin transformed the music of his homeland into piano masterpieces.

## DIAMOND HEAD

As a young boy, Frédéric studied at home instead of attending school. When he was thirteen, he enrolled at the Warsaw Lyceum, where his father taught. He took challenging courses, such as Greek and Latin. Frédéric was not a brilliant student, but he made many lifelong friends. During the summer, he was invited to his friends' country homes. His parents felt the fresh air was good for his health, and Frédéric loved the Polish countryside. He heard fiddlers playing folk music and shepherds playing their flutes. In 1824, he visited the small village of Szafarnia, where he nervously learned to ride a horse. He soon composed his first mazurka, the Polish dance.

Although it wasn't really his first piece, the Rondo in C Minor, published in 1825, was listed as Opus 1, or Chopin's first work. At age fifteen, he was invited to play for Alexander I, the Russian czar who ruled Warsaw. He performed on a new pipe organ in the Great Hall of the Warsaw Conservatory. Impressed by the talented teenager, the czar gave Frédéric a diamond ring. Years later, during hard times, the ring paid for Chopin's food and housing.

As a child, Frédéric sometimes experienced headaches, stomach pains, and fevers, according to biographers. He wasn't athletic, for his lungs were too weak. Chopin fell seriously ill when he was sixteen. His sister Emilia was also sick. In July 1826, Chopin, his mother, and two sisters, Emilia and Ludwika, took a stagecoach to Duszniki, a health resort in the mountains. The water from the mineral springs was said to cure lung diseases. In the clear mountain air, Chopin felt better. He gave two charity concerts, donating the money to orphans.

When he returned from Duszniki, Chopin entered the Warsaw Conservatory. He was already studying composition and music theory with Josef Elsner (1769–1832), the headmaster. Elsner taught him about harmony and counterpoint, or the art of combining more than one line of music. Yet hc gave Chopin the freedom to develop his own style. Chopin also took organ lessons from Wilhelm Würfel (1790–1832), a respected professor, and he joyfully played the organ every Sunday at a church in Warsaw. While Chopin was still a student, people began to take notice of his accomplishments.

A sad season came for the Chopin family in the spring of 1827. The health spa had not helped Emilia. She had grown sicker that winter and was probably suffering from tuberculosis, the contagious disease that attacks the lungs. At the time, doctors had no treatment for tuberculosis, and fourteen-year-old Emilia, already a talented writer, died on April 10, 1827. The words on her gravestone read, "Perished in the fourteenth spring of her life, like a flower in which blossomed the beautiful promise of fruit." Frédéric was devastated. After her death, the Chopin family moved to a new apartment in Warsaw.

## FULL OF PROMISE

When Chopin graduated from the conservatory in 1829, at age nineteen, his teachers knew he had an amazing talent. Elsner called his student a musical genius. Chopin wanted to see the world. In July, he and a few of his school friends traveled to Vienna, a city where many musicians gathered to listen to and compose contemporary music. A Viennese publisher offered to print Chopin's music if he gave a performance, so Chopin performed in Vienna to great success. Audiences shouted "Bravo!" and reviewers raved about the Polish musician. Chopin wrote to his parents, "I don't know why, but I appear to astonish the Germans, and I am astonished at their finding anything to be astonished at."

In August, Chopin traveled to Prague, Dresden, and other cities. He played in salons and met conductors, pianists, princesses, and Poles. After the whirlwind trip, Chopin returned to Warsaw and threw himself into writing two concertos for piano and orchestra. "Upstairs, there is a room which is supposed to serve my comfort, with stairs leading to it from the dressing room. Here I am to have my old piano and writing desk, and a nook where I can take refuge," he wrote to a friend. On March 17, 1830, people crowded the National Theater on Krasinski Square to hear Chopin's new Piano Concerto no. 2 in F Minor, a piece for piano and orchestra. Chopin told a friend that the slow Adagio movement was inspired by a singer he knew from school named Constantia Gladkowska. Nothing came of Chopin's romantic feelings, but the audience applauded the concerto.

Chopin spent the summer preparing his next concerto. "It is not meant to be loud, it's more of a romance, quiet, melancholy . . . It is a sort of meditation in beautiful spring weather, but by moonlight," he wrote to a friend. On October 11, he performed the Piano Concerto in E Minor at the National Theater, his final concert in Poland. Sad to leave his family but determined to build a career in Europe, Chopin set off for Vienna. His friend from school, Tytus Wojciechowksi, went with him. At the edge of Warsaw, Chopin's teacher, Elsner, saw them off with a farewell song for Chopin. Some say Elsner gave Chopin an urn with Polish soil. The whole world lay before him, but Chopin would always carry Poland with him in his heart.

# CHAPTER TWO

# City of Light

**D**ays after Chopin arrived in Vienna, a revolution erupted in Poland. The unhappy Poles took arms against their Russian rulers. The November Uprising, which broke out in Warsaw on November 29, 1830, was one of Poland's proudest moments. Chopin wished he could have been there like his friend Wojciechowksi, who had returned to Poland to join the rebels. Chopin worried about the safety of his family and friends in Poland during the uprising, but there was little he could do to protect them.

Despite his anguish at being away from Poland, Chopin composed a variety of music during his eight-month stay in Vienna. He wrote nine mazurkas, the Polish dances. He worked on a series of études, or studies. His Twelve Études, Opus 10, showed Chopin's growing maturity as a

Phillippe Benoist painted this view of the fountain of the Boulevard St. Martin in Paris around 1840. Artists, musicians, and writers, drawn by Paris's spirit of democracy and freedom, flocked to the city's cafés and boulevards.

composer. In writing them, he created something entirely new. One of the études, known as the "Black Key" Étude, uses only a piano's black keys. Chopin also wrote the Scherzo in B Minor, a strong piece, full of force and passion. Yet he wasn't earning money, and he still needed his father's financial support. Struggling to feed his family in war-torn Warsaw, Mikolaj sold the diamond ring given to the young Chopin and sent the money to his son.

On June 11, 1831, Chopin performed the Concerto in E Minor at the Kartnerthortheater in Vienna. It was a great success, but Chopin felt Vienna did not have enough to offer him as a composer. Unable to return to Poland now that its borders were closed, Chopin decided to go to Paris. On the way, he stopped in Stuttgart, Germany. He was there in September when news reached him that the

Russians had crushed the Polish uprising, and Warsaw had fallen. Chopin worried about his family. "Sometimes I can only groan, suffer, and pour out my despair at my piano! . . . I am right to be angry that I came into the world. What use is my existence to anyone?" he wrote in his notebook. Many times in his life, Chopin's moods darkened. His only way to beat a gloomy mood was to compose. Chopin's famous Étude no. 12 in C Minor, op. 10, known as the Revolutionary Étude, was written around this time.

## TO BREATHE PARISIAN AIR

Chopin arrived in Paris in September 1831. He was twenty-one years of age, ambitious, and eager to become a great composer and pianist. The capital of France, with its gray cobblestone streets and winding Seine River, was a vibrant city. It was an exciting time to be in Paris. The July Revolution had swept through France in 1830. The people threw out the conservative King Charles X. The new king, Louis Philippe, who promised a more democratic France, walked the streets in an ordinary suit, carrying a green umbrella. A sense of victory and hope filled the city.

Artists, musicians, and writers from across Europe flocked to the City of Light, seeking inspiration and intellectualism. They gathered in cafés and salons to debate ideas and argue politics. "To breathe the air of Paris preserves the soul," the Parisian novelist Victor Hugo would later write in *Les Miserables* (1867). His new novel, *The Hunchback of Notre Dame*, the tragic story of love between a gypsy girl and a cathedral bell ringer, had just been published. Hugo was a pioneer of the Romantic Movement, the artistic revolution bringing upheaval and rebirth to Paris. This rebellious era in art,

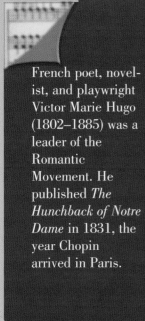

French poet, novelist, and playwright Victor Marie Hugo (1802–1885) was a leader of the Romantic Movement. He published *The Hunchback of Notre Dame* in 1831, the year Chopin arrived in Paris.

music, and writing was flourishing across Europe, but nowhere as intensely as Paris. Artists, musicians, and writers basked in a new opportunity to break free of the past and to celebrate their emotions. Chopin was caught by the fire of the movement but did not consider himself a romantic.

Chopin felt at home in Paris, since he was so warmly welcomed by the Polish community there. Some 10,000 people had fled Poland after Russians crushed the rebellion. This migration included artists, poets, doctors, and aristocrats. They still dreamed of a free Poland, and Paris became a center of the Polish independence movement. Although Chopin was invited to parties nearly every evening, he remained a struggling musician who worried about his future. "I am gradually launching myself on the world," he wrote to a friend, "but I have only one ducat [coin] in my pocket!"

Chopin had to climb several flights of stairs to his apartment at number 27, boulevard de la Poissonnière. It was the first of many apartments he took in the city. "I have a small room beautifully furnished in mahogany, with a balcony over the boulevard, from which I can see from Montmartre to the Pantheon and along the whole length of the fashionable quarter; many persons envy me, the view, but none my stairs," he wrote. As Chopin got to know Paris, he was amazed at what he witnessed. One could walk the streets in rags, yet still be respectable. He saw the greatest wealth and also terrible poverty.

One evening, Chopin was invited to the home of Baron James de Rothschild, one of the wealthiest men in France. A member of a powerful German banking family, he liked to spend his fortune supporting artists. Baron Rothschild and his wife, Betty, took Chopin under their wing. Betty became one of his first students. Years later, Chopin dedicated his Waltz in C-Sharp Minor to Madame Rothschild for her support.

A letter of introduction to the most famous pianist in the city, Friedrich Kalkbrenner, opened the doors of Paris's world of music to Chopin. Impressed by Chopin's talent, the older man offered to give him lessons. Even though Chopin declined, he greatly admired Kalkbrenner. "He is one whose shoe laces I am not worthy to untie," Chopin wrote in a letter. Kalkbrenner introduced Chopin to Camille Pleyel, the piano-maker and publisher. Pleyel bought Chopin a piano and arranged performances. As the months passed, Chopin became friends with many of Paris's musical stars, from the opera composer Gioacchino Rossini to the Hungarian pianist Franz Liszt.

A brilliant composer known for his wild flourishes, Liszt was almost the same age as Chopin. Like Chopin, Liszt left his country and found refuge in Paris, where he threw himself into composing, performing, and socializing. The two became friends and rivals. The Italian opera composer Vincenzo Bellino was another friend. Chopin loved the song of the opera, and it inspired many of his pieces. Chopin also was close to the French cellist Auguste Franchomme and even wrote a concerto for him.

Nearly every night, the musicians of Paris soaked up the city's culture. Chopin saw the opera *The Barber of Seville* by Rossini and heard Beethoven's Fifth Symphony, the big rage of the day. When the violinist Paganini came to Paris, Chopin attended every performance. After, Chopin and his friends dined on oysters, venison, and asparagus, and smoked cigars, wrote biographer Tad Szulc. Later, Chopin and his friends met in his candlelit apartment where they gathered around his piano. His friends were not all musicians, however. The German poet Heinrich Heine and the Polish poet Adam Mickewiez were frequently in Chopin's company, as was the painter Eugene Delacroix. While they all admired Chopin, he could be very critical of their talents.

## PARIS DEBUT

On February 26, 1832, Chopin made his Paris debut. The concert was on a Sunday night at the Salle Pleyel on the rue du Faubourg Saint Honoré, a hall owned by Pleyel. Many of Chopin's friends attended. Liszt was there with Felix Mendelssohn, a German pianist, conductor, and composer. Chopin played the Piano Concerto no. 2 in F Minor, his Mozart Variations, and other pieces. He swayed and rocked to his melodies, using the foot pedals generously and pouring himself into the music. The performance received warm praise, though some critics did not like his soft sound. Chopin bristled at the criticism; it made him doubt his talents.

Chopin gave several more concerts, but he truly disliked large audiences. "I am not suited for concert giving; the public intimidate me; their looks, only stimulated by curiosity, paralyze me; their strange faces oppress me; their breath stifles me," Chopin told a friend. Not only was he uncomfortable, Chopin felt his music was lost in a grand hall. He preferred intimate performances in the salons of friends.

Music was his life, yet Chopin also enjoyed luxury. He bought expensive furniture and covered it in the finest silk fabrics. When he went out at night, he wore elegant suits sewn by personal tailors. Chopin boasted a splendid figure, in a blue velvet jacket, black vest, white gloves, top hat fitted by a Paris hat maker, and black velvet cape with silver lining. His small shoes were handmade. Looking like a gentleman was important to Chopin, but it was expensive. "I have five lessons to give today. You think I am making a fortune? Carriages and white gloves cost more, and without them one would not be in good taste," he wrote to a friend. His father worried about his son's finances. Mikolaj wrote to Chopin, urging him to save his money.

## INSPIRING TEACHER

When a cholera epidemic swept across Paris in 1832, killing thousands, many of Chopin's wealthy friends left the city. Fewer parties and concerts filled the evenings. Chopin still had to earn money. Times were hard in Poland, and he couldn't take more money from his father.

Before the nineteenth century, composers relied on patrons, or wealthy nobles, who provided for them as long as they composed music. Mozart received support from the Archbishop of Salzburg, a leader of the Catholic Church, to launch his career in the 1760s, but these patronages were less common by the 1830s.

To help support his lavish lifestyle, Chopin taught piano. In his apartment, he saw as many as five students a day from October to May. From early morning through the afternoon, students trooped in and out of his rooms. He charged twenty gold francs for a lesson that lasted between forty-five minutes and one hour. If he liked them, or if they were especially gifted, he let them stay longer.

At first, his students were from the Polish community. The Rothschilds helped spread the word about Chopin's lessons. Princesses, baronesses, and duchesses from across Europe flocked to Chopin. Even a princess had to be prepared for her lesson. Although Chopin was patient, he was also passionate about music, and he became irritated by carelessness. He sat at a small upright piano, while the student sat at the large Pleyel piano. He stressed technique with his students. He made them use a metronome, a ticking time machine that keeps a steady rhythm. Students were taught how to position their hands, to play long and short notes differently, and to get their hands to move quickly.

He made them practice scales and exercises. Each finger, he believed, had a different strength and made a unique sound. Once a student mastered technique, he or she could move on to matters of style. Although Chopin liked to improvise, his students read from sheet music, often his own études and preludes. Chopin played the piece first, followed by his student. If the student didn't get the notes right the first time, Chopin would ask him or her to play it again. "Often the entire lesson passed without the pupil having played more than a few bars," wrote Carl Mikuli, Chopin's teaching assistant.

Chopin became a popular teacher. He was inspiring as well as strict. He urged his students to express themselves. "Put all your soul into it!" he would say, recalled one student, Moritz Karasowski. For Chopin, who loved opera, piano music was like song. He urged students to listen to the great operas for inspiration. One of his students, Emilie von Gretsch, recalled a lesson in 1844. "Yesterday at Chopin's I tried to play his Nocturnes," she wrote. Yet she found herself "unable to express the music as I heard it in my head." Chopin was patient and encouraging. "Be bolder, let yourself go more," Chopin told her.

## CHOPIN, THE BUSINESSMAN

Chopin also earned money by selling his sheet music. Sheet music was a thriving business in the 1830s. By then, many middle-class families had pianos in their homes and they wanted to play the latest pieces by popular composers. Soon after he came to Paris, Chopin signed a contract with Maurice Schlesinger, a Paris music publisher. In 1833, he arranged to publish a set of études and his popular Concerto in E Minor. Before long, his compositions were regularly published in Germany, England, and Spain.

Managing the publishing of his music was difficult. Chopin worried about how much he would be paid and when he would receive the money. A Polish school friend and musician, Julian Fontana, became his assistant. Fontana copied, edited, and sold Chopin's work. As his

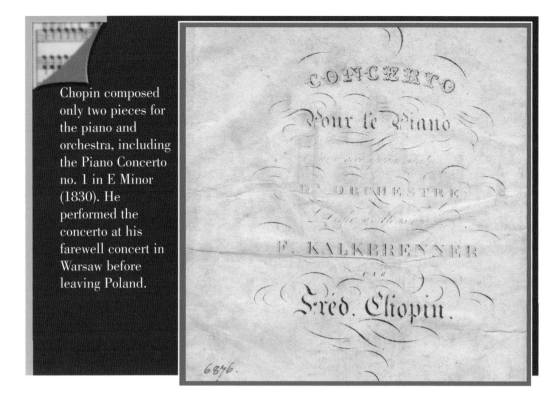

Chopin composed only two pieces for the piano and orchestra, including the Piano Concerto no. 1 in E Minor (1830). He performed the concerto at his farewell concert in Warsaw before leaving Poland.

fame grew, Chopin became more confident and demanded the sums he felt his music deserved. In 1839, he wrote to a publisher in Leipzig about twelve pieces that he would sell at 500 francs each. If he was offered anything less, he wouldn't sell them, he stated. In fact, Chopin's music sold well. He was able to rely on this income, though he never became wealthy. Many of his pieces were dedicated to wealthy supporters, good friends, and women he admired.

## A French Citizen

Between composing, teaching, and watching the opera, Chopin's life in Paris turned out more wonderful than he had ever dreamed it would. "If I ever had everything at once, it's now, in Paris," he wrote. He was amazed at all that had happened. "I have got into the highest society; I sit with ambassadors, princes, ministers; and even don't know how it came about, because I did not try for it," he wrote to an old friend. Yet Chopin was homesick and missed his family in Poland. He had given up his Russian passport, so he could not return to a Poland under the czar.

Still, Paris had been Chopin's home for years, so he became a full-fledged French citizen in August 1835. With his new French passport, he was able to travel freely. He took a stagecoach on a ten-day journey to meet his parents in Carlsbad, Bohemia, now the Czech Republic. They were vacationing at the health spa and did not know their son would be there. Overjoyed to see one another, they spent four weeks together. Even then, Chopin kept composing. By the end of the summer, he had finished a new waltz. Chopin wrote to his sisters in Warsaw, "We are happier than we can describe. We hug each other and hug again; what more can we do; what a pity we are all not together." He did not know that he would never see his parents again.

## YOUNG LOVE

On his journey back to Paris, Chopin stopped in the historic city of Dresden and stayed with the Wodzinskas, a Polish family. In Warsaw, the three sons had roomed with the Chopins while they attended the lyceum. The family also had a sixteen-year-old daughter, Maria. She was educated and played the piano. She admired Chopin and loved listening to him play. The two took long walks and talked a lot. Gradually, their friendship became serious. Now in his mid-twenties, Chopin had never had a serious romantic relationship.

He made another stop, in Leipzig, where he met Clara Wieck, a talented young pianist and composer.

## Pianoforte

The piano was barely 100 years old when Chopin was born. An Italian harpsichord maker named Bartolomeo Cristofori built the first piano in 1709. He made important changes from the harpsichord, which had strings that were plucked by a feather to make sound. For his new instrument, Cristofori used hammers covered in leather to strike the keys. He called the instrument "piano e forte," or "soft and loud," because players could control the loudness of the notes by touch—a feat not possible with the harpsichord. His wooden instrument was large and shaped like a wing, similar to a grand piano today. You can see a Cristofori pianoforte at the Metropolitan Museum of Art in New York City.

Chopin's pianoforte was not like the modern piano. The early pianofortes had only four octaves. An octave is the twelve-note scale. By Chopin's day, pianos had six and a half octaves. Modern pianos have seven and a half octaves. Also, Chopin's pianoforte had two pedals—the sostenuto, or sustained loud pedal, and the una corda, or soft pedal. Chopin used the pedals to expand the tone of the instrument. Some modern pianos have three pedals, including the middle pedal, developed in the 1870s, which allows pianists to hold notes longer.

The Pleyel family, a group of prominent Paris piano makers, made Chopin's favorite pianofortes. Pleyel instruments were known to have a smooth, sweet sound. Camille Pleyel, the son of the company's founder and composer Ignacio Pleyel, was a good friend to Chopin. He published many of his compositions and supported him in Paris.

Female musicians were rare in the 1830s, and Wieck was considered one of the finest pianists in Europe. Chopin is said to have declared that Wieck was the only woman in Germany who could play his music. He also visited the German composers Felix Mendelssohn and Robert Schumann, a student of Clara's father. The musicians played for each other and became friends. Schumann, who later married Clara, gave up a career as a concert pianist after injuring his finger. He turned to composing and writing about musicians. One of his favorite people to write about was Chopin. After he heard Chopin's Mozart Variations, Schumann wrote, "Hats off, gentlemen, a genius!" His generous praise boosted Chopin's confidence.

Meanwhile, Chopin couldn't forget Maria. When he returned to Paris, Chopin wrote to Maria and her mother. They quickly responded. Chopin dedicated his latest waltz to Maria. The following summer, Chopin visited the family in Marienbad, a health spa in what is now the Czech Republic. The two wanted to get married, but Maria's father disapproved, fearing Chopin's poor health or unsteady income. After Chopin's return to Paris, his letters to Maria were not answered. Chopin was so upset that he traveled to London to forget Maria, but he remained miserable and returned to Paris. Until his death years later, Chopin kept a bundle of Maria's letters, wrapped in string and tied with a note that read "my sorrow," in Polish. Despite this devastating loss, Chopin soon would meet another woman who would steal his heart.

# CHAPTER THREE

## An Unusual Romance

One evening in the fall of 1836, Chopin's good friend Franz Liszt, the musician, invited him to a party at the Hotel de France on the rue Laffitte. Liszt and his companion, Countess Maria d'Agoult, were celebrating their return to Paris after a stay in Switzerland. They invited a small group of friends to their salon. During the evening, Chopin sat down at the piano. As he played, one of the guests watched closely. She did not look like the ordinary Parisian woman, for she wore men's clothing and smoked a cigar.

The dark-haired woman also used a man's name and sometimes wore a top hat. Chopin learned she was the writer George Sand. By 1836, Sand had written several popular novels about love and romance. Parisian women

George Sand, the pseudonym of Amandine-Aurore-Lucile Dudevant, wrote popular romantic novels about the working class, and supported democratic causes in nineteenth-century Paris. She was the love of Chopin's life.

couldn't wait to read her next steamy tale. Sand was also active in revolutionary politics. At a time when women were invisible in public life, she spoke her mind. "Her first books shocked people, [and] her early opinions were greeted with storms," wrote biographer Rene Doubin. Sand was determined to cut her own path in life and never apologized for behavior. "I ask the support of no one, neither to kill someone for me, to gather a bouquet, to correct a proof, or to go with me to the theater. I go there by myself . . . If ever I have a name, it will be entirely of my own making," wrote Sand in a letter to her friend Charles Didion in 1836.

## A RESTLESS CHILDHOOD

Unlike Chopin, Sand came from a broken family. She was born Amandine-Aurore-Lucile Dupin in Paris on July 1, 1804, to Sophie and Maurice Dupin. Maurice was from an aristocratic family, while Sophie's father ran a pool hall and sold finches and canaries in a Paris square. "My mother was a poor child on the old streets of Paris," wrote Sand. Aurore's childhood was not easy, for Sophie had little patience for parenting. When Aurore was four years of age, the family traveled with Maurice, then an officer in the French army, to Spain. Led by Napoléon, the French had conquered Spain. When the Spanish people rose up in rebellion, Aurore and her family had to flee. They nearly starved to death on their way back to France. Aurore's baby brother died after they got home, and Maurice died soon after.

Sophie returned to Paris, while Aurore stayed with her grandmother at her estate in Nohant in Berry. The estate, some 180 miles (280 kilometers) south of Paris, was like a paradise, with peacocks in the gardens, grazing sheep, and deep woods to explore. Sand grew close to her grandmother, who raised her as a polished young woman with a love of reading. As a teenager, Sand spent two and a half years in a convent in Paris. She almost became a nun before her grandmother took her back to Nohant.

At sixteen years of age, Sand married Casimir Dudevant, a soldier and baron, and her name became Aurore Dudevant. The couple had a son and daughter, Maurice and Solange, but the couple was unhappy and soon separated. Sand lived as an independent woman and single mother. She pursued a career as a writer in Paris, often criticizing the government in newspapers. In 1831, she published a novel, *Rose et Blanche*, under the pen name J. Sand. She wrote it with her friend Jules Sandeau. Her next novel, *Indiana*, was all her own. Her publisher suggested using "Sand" again. He also told her to invent a

The unconventional George Sand admired Chopin's talent and encouraged him to compose, even when he was ill. She once said, "He made a simple instrument speak the language of infinity."

first name. She chose "George," which in Greek means "a man of the earth," to reflect her happy years in Nohant. She hoped that a man's name would help the novel sell.

## AN UNLIKELY PAIR

Chopin's talent and personality intrigued Sand. He was handsome, with thick, wavy light brown hair, a shapely nose, and deep eyes. True, he was thin and frail. Chopin never weighed more than 100 pounds. Still, he cut a fine figure, and Sand, like many women in Paris, was fascinated by his sensitive look and gentle manner. In contrast, Chopin, who was six years younger, did not know what to think about Sand. He is said to have told a friend that she didn't even look like a woman! Sand and Chopin met a few more times in the next months, and in the spring of 1838, they fell in love.

Sand and Chopin made an unlikely pair. Sand was strong, healthy, and energetic. Chopin, already sick with coughs and fevers by 1838, was pale, thin, and frail. Sand was outgoing and talkative, while Chopin, whom she lovingly referred to as her "dear skeleton," was quieter, moody, and reserved. He didn't like to talk about himself or voice strong opinions. Even Chopin's closest friends rarely heard him express his true feelings, wrote Franz Liszt in his book, *The Life of Chopin.* Nor did Sand and Chopin agree about politics. Chopin was more cautious and conservative. Although he wanted a free Poland, he was not active in politics. He admired the French monarchy and gave private concerts for the king. Sand fought for democracy and the rights of workers and the poor. She despised the monarchy.

Yet they shared a love for art, literature, and music. Most important, they respected each other. "My lady has just finished a magnificent article . . . One must read it; it gladdens the heart," Chopin wrote to a friend in 1839. Sand admired Chopin's music as well. "He made a single instrument speak the language of infinity. He was often able to condense in ten lines that a child could play poems of immense elevation, dreams of unequaled emotion," Sand wrote in her autobiography. They always supported each other's work.

Sand saw that Chopin's health was becoming more fragile. She became his loving nurse and companion. In the fall of 1838, he fell very ill. At the same time, Sand's young son, Maurice, had rheumatism, a painful joint disease. Sand decided they needed to escape Paris's harsh winter and spend time in a warm, sunny climate. Chopin, Sand, and her two children left Paris for Majorca, an island off the coast of Spain in the Mediterranean Sea. To pay for the trip, Chopin signed a contract to write a set of preludes for Camille Pleyel, who agreed to pay him 2,000 francs for the compositions. Before long, they all boarded a boat headed for Spain.

## WINTER IN MAJORCA

At first, Majorca seemed perfect. The rugged island was covered in palm trees, fig trees, orchards, and roses. Chopin was thrilled with Majorca's beauty. "A sky like turquoise, a sea like lapis lazuli, mountains like emerald, air like heaven," he described to a friend. But the weather quickly turned rainy and cold, and Chopin grew disenchanted. They had trouble finding a place to stay and then finding furniture. Pleyel sent a piano, but it took weeks to arrive. Sand later wrote a book about the trip. She described the people of Majorca as unfriendly, especially after they learned Chopin was ill. They suspected he had consumption, or tuberculosis, though the doctors had not yet diagnosed him. In Spain, tuberculosis was considered as contagious as the plague. People with the disease were isolated so they did not infect others. In France, tuberculosis was less feared. Parisians often considered it a "romantic" condition to which one was born.

As soon as he heard Chopin's persistent cough, their landlord turned them out of the house they had rented and burned their sheets. They even had to pay for their beds, which the landlord planned to burn, too. They found refuge in an old stone monastery on a hilltop called Valldemosa, where they lived in a three-room monk's cell that looked out on a garden of lemon and orange trees. From the terrace, Chopin could see the sea. Sand spent her days reading to her children, writing, preparing

# A Portrait, Divided

The French romantic artist Eugene Delacroix painted the finest portrait of Chopin and George Sand in 1838. Known for his brash colors, Delacroix was a leading artist. Born in the French Alps, he came to Paris as a student. Classical painters, like John Paul Rubens, influenced him greatly, but he was looking to the future. Delacroix used short paint strokes and contrasting colors to express themes of romanticism, liberty, and action.

One of Delacroix's best-known paintings is the *Massacre at Chios*, which portrays the Greek struggle for independence from Turkey. In 1830, the artist painted *Liberty Leading the People*, to celebrate the July Revolution. A young woman, representing Liberty, holds a gun and the flag of the French Revolution as she leads people over injured soldiers and fallen protesters. The man with the black top hat may have been Delacroix himself.

Delacroix and Chopin became close friends. In his journal, Delacroix wrote about pleasant evenings spent together. He often visited Chopin when he was ill. On April 7, 1849, the artist wrote, "Went with Chopin for his drive about half past three . . . We talked of music. It seemed to cheer him." Delacroix

Artist Eugene Delacroix was a close friend of Chopin's and painted a portrait of the composer and George Sand in 1838, which later became well known. However, the painting was later divided. Chopin's portrait hangs in the Louvre in Paris.

even moved a piano into his studio so Chopin could play. Delacroix's painting of his friends, never finished, shows Chopin at the piano while George Sand listens. The painting was cut in half after Delacroix's death. Chopin's portrait hangs in the Louvre in Paris, while Sand's is in the Ordrupgaard Collection in Copenhagen, Denmark. No one knows why the portrait was cut. The seller may have hoped to make more money on two paintings, instead of one.

meals, and taking care of Chopin. Maurice, a talented artist, loved to paint and sketch, and Solange played in the hills. Chopin spent his days and nights at the piano.

The cold, rainy weather was bad for Chopin's health. The monastery was damp, and the fire emitted too much smoke. Chopin coughed blood and could barely lift himself out of bed. "I have been as sick as a dog these last two weeks," he wrote to Julian Fontana, his Polish editor. Three doctors came to see him. "One sniffed at what I spat up, the second tapped where I spat it from, the third poked about and listened how I spat it," he wrote. They could do little to help. He had to convince them not to bleed his veins, then a common treatment. Sand milked a goat and tried to keep him nourished. Chopin was also agitated and nervous. He found himself imagining things; the monastery seemed full of ghosts. "I would find him, at ten in the evening, pale at his piano, his eyes haggard, his hair standing almost on end. It would take him several moments to recognize us," wrote Sand in her autobiography.

## RAIN AND PRELUDES

Even illness did not stop Chopin from composing. He completed some of his finest pieces that winter, including the 24 Preludes, op. 28. The preludes are based loosely on Bach's Well-Tempered Clavier. Like Bach's masterpiece, each of Chopin's preludes is in a different key and expresses a different mood. The Prelude no. 15 in D-flat Major, op. 28 is sometimes called the "Raindrop" Prelude. The repeated A-flat note in the left hand seems to mimic the rain that fell in Majorca. In early 1839, he mailed the preludes to Fontana. He asked Fontana to dedicate the preludes to

Pleyel. Chopin also worked on a ballade, two polonaises, and a scherzo.

Finally, in February, Sand and Chopin decided to return to France. On the boat, Chopin was pale, and he was again spitting blood. Sand arranged a stop in Marseilles on the French coast. Chopin was too weak to travel farther. While waiting for his health to improve, Chopin wrote to Fontana, instructing him about selling the new music he had written. Sand had her own project. "My Angel is finishing a new novel: *Gabriel*. Today she is writing in bed all day," Chopin wrote to a friend in April. When Chopin was better, they returned to Sand's home in Nohant. "The village is beautiful: nightingales, skylarks . . ." he wrote soon after he arrived. Over the summer, he composed the Sonata no. 2 in B-flat Minor, op. 35, one of his finest works. The third movement is the famous "Funeral March," which is often played today at funerals. Chopin also worked on new mazurkas and a nocturne, his serene song of the night.

In October, Chopin returned to Paris. He was glad to be home and among his friends. For the next few years, Sand and Chopin lived nearby in separate apartments in Paris during the winters. They were devoted to each other and to their work. Most summers, they traveled to Nohant for rest. The two remained together for eight years, but they never married. These were some of Chopin's happiest and most productive times.

# CHAPTER FOUR

## Poet of the Piano

On the evening of April 26, 1841, a stream of horse-drawn carriages stopped at the Salle Pleyel, the concert hall in Paris where Chopin was performing. Stepping out from the carriages were "the most elegant ladies, the most fashionable young men, the most famous artists, the richest financiers, the most illustrious lords . . ." reported the composer Franz Liszt, who was there that evening. No longer a newcomer to Paris, Chopin was famous. As Lizst remarked, according to biographer Ates Organ, he was a skilled virtuoso, a piano expert, an artist—"he was all this and much more; he was Chopin."

Most of the people at the concert were Chopin's friends. In the hall, a grand piano stood on the platform. The audience had paid 20 francs for a ticket, and everyone

Chopin played for King Louis Philippe at the Tuileries Palace in 1841. Although his close friends resented the monarchy and advocated a democracy, Chopin was honored to perform for the king.

tried to get the closest seat available. A performance by the shy pianist, even for a group of friends, was unusual. Chopin agreed to do it only because George Sand had insisted. She thought a big concert would do him good, and he needed the money.

Chopin chose some of his most daring compositions, pieces that veered far from the staid, classical music of the past. He played his preludes, études, nocturnes, and mazurkas. As always, Chopin's music was original. With his harmonies, moody melancholies, and flights of emotion, Chopin created music that was daring. "In truth nothing equals the lightness, the sweetness with which this artist preludes on the piano . . . [his work is] full of originality, distinction and grace. Chopin is a pianist apart, who should not be and cannot be compared with anyone," wrote a French music critic, according to biographer Ates Organ.

## A ROMANTIC COMPOSER

Chopin was a composer of the Romantic Age, a period in art, music, literature, and social thought that lasted from the late 1700s to the mid-1800s. The Romantics were rebels who sought new freedoms. As political revolutions uprooted monarchies across Europe, the Romantics rebelled against old ideas about art and creativity. They rejected the order, harmony, and balance admired in the 1700s, ignored realism, and instead tapped into their emotions, dreams, and imaginations. Romantic artists celebrated nature, patriotism, passion, and the mystical world. The poet "will follow wheresoever he can find an atmosphere of sensation in which to move his wings," wrote the Romantic British poet William Wordsworth. Writers such as Wordsworth and John Keats in England, Victor Hugo and Honore Balzac in France, and Walt Whitman and Edgar Allen Poe in the United States led the movement forward. In painting, Chopin's friend Delacroix used brilliant color and daring strokes to express great feeling.

Chopin's musical friends and rivals were swept up in Romanticism. They respected the composers of earlier generations, such as Bach, Mozart, and especially Beethoven, who died when Chopin was seventeen. Yet they yearned for new musical expression and used richer harmonies and changing tempos. Women swooned at concerts by Liszt, the dashing Hungarian pianist. His subtle, intimate music was often inspired by poetry and literature. Robert Schumann, the German composer, used new rhythms and harmonies in his short piano pieces and long symphonies. Emotional themes were also popular. The French composer Hector Berlioz's Fantastic Symphony in 1830 tells the story of an artist who poisons himself with opium because he has been hurt in love.

## PURE MUSIC

Unlike his friends, Chopin was not usually inspired by nature or poetry. His compositions were pure music. He gave them simple titles, such as Mazurka, Nocturne, or Concerto. Still, some people say Chopin was the ultimate Romantic composer. He transformed traditional music forms by using new harmonies, rhythms, and a soaring lyricism, or songlike quality. The scherzo, for example, is usually a light, musical joke. But Chopin's scherzos are far from funny. Difficult for all but the best pianist, his scherzos feel tragic. "How is gravity to clothe itself if jest goes about in dark veils?" asked Schumann. If Chopin's scherzos were gloomy, then his serious pieces were even darker.

Chopin broke new ground in many ways. Dissonance, or the sound of notes that conflict and seem disagreeable, added tension to his music. He used counterpoint to set in motion two or more melodies at the same time. Meanwhile, his tempo was never predictable. Some people even said Chopin didn't know how to follow time. Actually, he used a technique called tempo rubato, or robbed time, to allow more freedom. He purposely held notes for different lengths of time than called for by the meter signature, which emphasized the notes. The meter signature tells how many beats in a measure and which note gets one beat.

Chopin also gave the left hand a more important role. One legend says Chopin urged students to play freely with

Chopin autographed this mazurka score, written in Paris in 1834. He often wrote several versions of his pieces, which he dedicated to friends. Chopin's sheet music sold across Europe, and his fame grew.

their right hand, but let the left one act as a conductor and keep time. Using the foot pedal to sustain the bass notes while the piano sang like an opera aria was another Chopin innovation. "Chopin, in other words, sounds like no one else," wrote biographer Jim Samson.

## THE POLONAISE

In June, Chopin and Sand left Paris. He wrote much of his music during the peaceful summers at Sand's home in Nohant. He sat at the piano to compose in the morning and evening, even when he wasn't well. Sand said he got his inspiration while walking in the gardens or while playing. Sometimes he stayed up all night, pacing his room. Chopin revised his music again and again. Even when he felt it was finished, he did not write down the music in final form. Instead, Julian Fontana and others copied and edited his music to sell to publishers. For these reasons, many of his pieces have several versions.

During the summer of 1841, Chopin finished one of his finest pieces, Polonaise in F-sharp Minor, op. 44. The polonaise is a stately Polish court dance. Like many Romantics, Chopin celebrated his nationality. His most famous Polish works are his lively mazurkas and grand polonaises. The mazurka is the dance of the peasants; the polonaise is the dance of the courts. Chopin's Polonaise in F-sharp Minor was dramatic and original, and nothing like the court dance. Liszt said it felt like the ominous air before a hurricane. Soon after, Chopin wrote Polonaise in A-flat Major, op. 53, known as the "Heroic" Polonaise, filled with Polish patriotism and pride.

Chopin also wrote nocturnes, a word meaning "night." The nocturne is a one-movement piece filled with emotion. An Irishman named John Fields wrote the first nocturnes in 1813, but Chopin took the form to new heights. Chopin's nocturnes are quiet and melancholic, yet full of spirit. Chopin's nocturnes are also lyrical, with amazing harmonies and soaring arpeggios, the scattered notes of a chord moving up and down the keyboard.

In fact, Chopin's spirits seemed to soar and fall, just like his music. That autumn, after he completed a new piece, he wrote to Fontana, "Today I completed the Fantaisie—the sky is beautiful and my heart is heavy— but this does not matter. If it were otherwise, then my existence would have been of no use to anyone. Let us wait until after death." This lament was not unusual for Chopin. He often struggled with despair, even when his career was thriving. Some biographers believe Chopin suffered from manic depression or perhaps another mental illness.

## A ROYAL CONCERT

Back in Paris, Chopin and Sand attended the opera and the theater, and met friends for late-night gatherings. In December 1841, Chopin was invited to perform for King Louis Philippe and his court at the Tuileries Palace. The grand palace, with its long, narrow buildings and courtyards on the Seine, had been home to French royalty since the sixteenth century. This was a grand occasion. Unlike Sand and many of his Polish friends, Chopin admired the king, and he was honored to play for his court. Sand couldn't understand his point of view. Her concern was for the ordinary people of France. She wanted equal rights and democracy for all. Nevertheless, the performance was a success, and the king paid Chopin and gave him a set of fine porcelain.

Yet the shadow cast by Chopin's illnesses was darkening. He coughed constantly. The winter cold made him feel worse. One of Chopin's closest Polish friends, a doctor named Jan Matuszyriski, believed that he suffered from tuberculosis. For several years, he and Chopin shared apartments in Paris. In April 1842, Matuszyriski died of the disease. He had the same doctor as Chopin, and this seemed a bad omen. No one would say Chopin had tuberculosis, but his health was deteriorating.

After a busy spring, Chopin returned to Nohant for the summer. He and Sand were glad to have a visitor, their friend Delacroix. The painter brought his cat, Cupid. Sand made a studio for him in one of the stables. The painter even offered to tutor Sand's son, Maurice, who liked to draw. During his visit, Delacroix painted Saint Anne, the patron saint of Nohant, and gave the painting to the village church. On summer holidays, Chopin and

Delacroix watched villagers dance to the song of the bagpipe. Just as he enjoyed the music of the Polish peasants, Chopin liked this entertainment. At night, while Delacroix read in his room, he could hear Chopin at the piano. His music drifted into the night. Delacroix deeply admired Chopin. "God's presence descends from his finger-tips," he wrote, according to biographer Benita Eisler. "Of all that I've known, he's the only true artist among us." Unfortunately, Chopin, often critical of his friends, did not care for Delacroix's paintings.

When the weather grew cooler, Chopin returned to Paris. He and Sand had moved to separate apartments in the Square d'Orleans. With a courtyard between them, the two remained close. Artists, musicians, and political activists lived there, too, and Chopin invited guests in the evenings. But winter brought illness again, and Chopin weakened, prompting his doctor to try a new treatment, which brought some success, and Chopin improved.

Chopin wrote several famous pieces that winter. One of his finest was the Ballade no. 4 in F Minor, op. 52. Some people think that Chopin's ballades tell stories and that they were inspired by the poems of his friend, the Polish poet Adam Mickiewicz. This ballade lasts only about twelve minutes, but it is difficult to play and presents a challenge to pianists. With much music still left to write, Chopin wasn't giving in to his worsening illness.

# CHAPTER FIVE
# The Last Mazurka

In May 1844, Chopin learned his father had died in Warsaw. Chopin had seen Mikolaj Chopin, who was seventy-two, only once since leaving Warsaw in 1831. They were very close, and Chopin felt his loss deeply. Chopin's cough worsened, and he seemed to be slipping away. George Sand wrote to Chopin's sisters, urging them to visit their brother. "You are certain to find my dear boy very weak and much changed since the last time you saw him!" wrote Sand, according to biographer Herbert Weinstock. Ludwika and her husband soon arrived in France and spent three weeks with Chopin in Nohant.

He spent quiet days with his sister and worked on his new Sonata no. 3 in B Minor, op. 58. In all, Chopin wrote four sonatas, including one for cello. He created a new form for the classical sonata. The Sonata in B Minor has four movements, finishing with the rapid presto movement. Many people say this sonata was Chopin's last masterpiece.

By summer's end, Chopin improved, yet everyone could see his time was short. In the next years, Chopin's life was often halted by illness. He became weaker. Many doctors were called to his home, but none could cure his coughs and fevers. In between the bouts of illness, however, he felt fine. He and Sand attended concerts and visited friends. He even went on a camping trip, sleeping out of doors.

One of Chopin's most famous pieces, the Waltz no. 1 in D-flat Major, op. 64, was written in 1845 and 1846. One story says Sand was at home in her Paris apartment, watching her dog chase its tail. Chopin wrote "le valse du petit chien," or the "waltz of the little dog." Known as The Minute Waltz, it is played by many beginning piano students. As a matter of fact, the waltz takes only two minutes to play, and like most of Chopin's work, it isn't an easy piece.

Despite their mutual respect, the two artists were not getting along. Gradually, their life together unraveled. Sand's new novel, *Lucrezia Floriani*, sparked controversy in 1846. In the book, a delicate artist named Prince Karol de Roswald falls in love with Lucrezia, an older actress. The match ends tragically, and Prince Karol kills Lucrezia. The book was published, chapter-by-chapter, in a Paris newspaper. Franz Liszt was one of many friends shocked by the book's echo of the real lives of Sand and Chopin.

When people dance the mazurka, a traditional dance of Poland, they stamp their feet and click their heels. Chopin reinvented the mazurka as fine piano music, but kept its strong spirit.

## A FINAL BREAK

Chopin spent one last summer at Nohant in 1846. He wrote intensely, finishing new sets of nocturnes and mazurkas, and the Sonata in G Minor for Piano and Cello, op. 65, for his friend, the cellist Auguste Franchomme. By the following spring, he was seriously ill. Though he recovered within weeks, Sand knew that every attack made him weaker. Chopin's illnesses, adding to their intense personalities, strained their relationship further. The couple bitterly disagreed about Sand's children. Chopin was close to Sand's daughter, Solange, but the teenager, who was about to be married, and her mother had a stormy relationship. Chopin was caught between them. Sand's son, Maurice, and Chopin fought as well.

In 1847, Sand and Chopin parted. Sand was ready to move on with her life, but she still cared for Chopin. "I have been repaid for my years of vigil, anguish, and devotion with years of tenderness, trust, and gratitude," wrote Sand in her autobiography. Meanwhile, Chopin struggled to live on his own.

## REVOLUTION OF 1848

While Chopin's personal life was chaotic, Paris was boiling. After winning some freedoms in 1830, the French had years of relative peace under King Louis Philippe and his July Monarchy. However, the poor and middle class were still not allowed to vote. Poor harvests and a sinking economy put people out of work in 1847. The king was becoming unpopular. Across Europe, democratic revolutions were unfolding, led by the middle class against old monarchies. This period is called the Springtime of Nations.

A bitterly cold winter settled on Paris in 1848, and the Seine froze. Chopin fell sick with a "frightful grippe," or flu, as he wrote in a letter. Still, he prepared for a concert, set for February 16. Writing his family, Chopin recalled, "My friends came one morning and told me that I must give a concert, that I need not worry over anything, only sit down and play." His friend Camille Pleyel arranged for flowers to fill the Salle Pleyel. Chopin performed the last three movements of his new cello sonata with his friend, the cellist Franchomme. People were amazed at his soft touch and delicate tone.

Outside the concert hall, the world was turning upside down. On February 22, riots erupted in the Parisian streets. Fed up with King Louis Phillipe, protesters set fires, turned over barricades, and felled trees. Soldiers fired into crowds. Louis Philippe gave up the throne, and the French royal family fled to England. The French people established the Second Republic and gave everyone the right to vote. Amid the chaos, the concert halls closed, and wealthy Parisians fled the city. Unable to teach or perform, Chopin struggled. He was sick again, and Paris was paralyzed. Chopin met Sand on the steps of a friend's house in March. They exchanged polite greetings, but that was all. This was the last time they spoke.

One of Chopin's students came to his rescue. Jane Stirling, a Scottish woman, was a favorite pupil. He even dedicated two nocturnes to her. Stirling and her sister, Katherine Erskine, invited Chopin to London and promised to help him find work. He decided to leave Paris so he could perform and teach again.

## Fog and Concerts

In April, Chopin took a ferry across the English Channel, then a coach to London. He moved into a flat at 48 Dover Street, furnished with three grand pianos. Chopin taught and played small concerts in people's homes for a fee. He also went to concerts and parties. He was thrilled to see the Swedish singer Jenny Lind, known as "the Swedish Nightingale," in several concerts. "She sings with extreme purity and certainty, and her piano notes are steady, and as even as a hair," he wrote to a friend. Lind became fond of Chopin, too. She later visited him in Paris and gave a big donation to a tuberculosis hospital. Some historians speculate that Lind even fell in love with Chopin.

In June, Chopin was invited to play for the British queen, Victoria, and her husband, Prince Albert, at the home of a duchess. "The Duchess presented me to the

Queen, who was very amiable and talked to me twice. Prince Albert came up to the pianoforte. Everyone told me both these things are very rare," wrote Chopin to his family. He met lords and ladies, and he gave lessons to their children. Still he was uncomfortable, for he did not speak much English, and London's fog made his cough worse. Gradually, he became discouraged. He was not earning enough money, and his health had worsened.

When summer came, Londoners left the city, and Chopin had little work. Stirling suggested he go to Scotland. He left on a twelve-hour journey to Edinburgh. In Scotland, he stayed in people's castles and the homes of aristocrats, where he was paid for concerts. Although Chopin was tired, he gave several concerts in September, including one in Glasgow, Scotland. A near tragedy occurred when a carriage he was riding in fell off the road and he was injured. Shortly after, he returned to London.

Chopin held his last public concert on November 16, 1848, at London's Guildhall. The concert raised money for Polish refugees. Chopin could play for only an hour because he had little strength. Chopin wrote to an old school friend that he missed Poland. "I scarcely remember anymore how they sing at home. That world slips away from me somehow; I forget, I have no more strength [crossed out]; if I rise a little, I fall again, lower than ever."

## FINAL FAREWELLS

In late November, Chopin returned to Paris. His friends were shocked at his frail appearance. Doctors could do little for him. By now, his diagnosis was tuberculosis. Today, historians speculate that Chopin may have had other chronic diseases, such as cystic fibrosis or emphysema. In any case, no treatment was effective. Fortunately, his friends did not forget him. The Rothschilds gave him money. Jane Stirling also sent money and came to nurse him. Though his greatest music was completed, Chopin worked when he could. The last piece he composed was a mazurka in F minor.

In June, Chopin wrote to his sister Ludwika in Poland, "If you can come. Do. I am ill, and no doctor will do as much for me as some of you. If you are short of money, borrow some . . ." Ludwika arrived in Paris in August. She sat by her brother's bedside and tried to keep him comfortable. In the final weeks, he declared he wanted his unpublished works to be burned. Fortunately, many pieces survived to be published after his death.

Even on his deathbed, Chopin received visitors. The wealthy French and Polish ladies who adored him came for their last respects. Delacroix stopped by almost every evening, sad to see his friend weakening. On August 3, Chopin wrote, "I gasp, cough, and am drowsy. I do nothing. I want nothing." The Polish poet Cyprian Kamil Norwid remembered his last visit. "The artist's sister sat at his side, strangely like him in profile . . . He, in the shadow of a deep bed with curtains, propped up on pillows, and wrapped in a shawl, looked very beautiful, as always . . ." Chopin could barely speak between coughing fits. Shortly after this day, Chopin was moved to a sunnier apartment at Place Vendóme 12.

He died early in the morning of October 17, 1849. Ludwika was by his side. His suffering was over. Delacroix wrote in his journal, "After luncheon I learned of the death of poor Chopin . . . What a loss! What miserable rogues fill the marketplace while that beautiful soul burns out!" He drew a sketch of Chopin, with a wreath on his head, like the famous Italian poet Dante. Chopin's obituary read, "A member of the family of Warsaw by nationality, a Pole in his heart and a citizen of the world by his talent has passed from this world."

Chopin had requested Mozart's Requiem at his funeral. Mozart was writing the Requiem, one of his greatest pieces, when he died in 1791. The Requiem has parts for female singers, but women could not sing in the Church of the Madeleine, where the service was planned. Two weeks passed before the church agreed to allow the female singers. On October 30, 3,000 people gathered for Chopin's funeral. Two of his preludes were also performed.

Chopin was buried at the Père Lachaise cemetery in Paris next to his friend, the Italian opera composer Bellini. At his request, Ludwika carried his heart back to Warsaw to the Church of the Holy Cross, where it was placed in a pillar. The church was bombed during World War II, but Chopin's heart was removed to a safe place. When the war ended, it was returned.

## PIANO SOUL

Even today, Chopin's grave in Paris has fresh flowers every day. Loved and admired in his lifetime, Chopin is considered one of the greatest composers of all time. "The piano bard, the piano rhapsodist, the piano mind, the piano soul is Chopin," said the Russian pianist and composer Anton Rubinstein, who was born in 1829 and often played Chopin's music. Chopin made the piano a solo instrument and gave it an entirely new expression. He created "a revolution in the language of music and with only one instrument," as Sand once said. Students and professionals play Chopin's nocturnes. Chopin societies

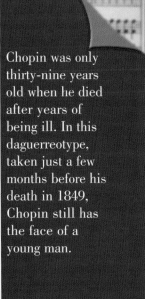

Chopin was only thirty-nine years old when he died after years of being ill. In this daguerreotype, taken just a few months before his death in 1849, Chopin still has the face of a young man.

sponsor concerts and competitions and fund research throughout the world.

While Chopin struggled to support himself, his original manuscripts are now very valuable. In 2004, the Polish Ministry of Culture bought a three-page manuscript of his Étude no. 4 in C-sharp Minor, op. 10 from the Sotheby's auction house in London. Poland paid 300,000 pounds (more than $530,000) for the signed manuscript, now at the Frederick Chopin Society in Warsaw.

Poland considers Chopin to be among its finest musicians. His birthplace in Zelazowa Wola is a popular destination for admirers. The cottage is now a museum, and each summer, Chopin's nocturnes and preludes are performed. The Frederic Chopin Airport in Warsaw is Poland's largest airport—a tribute to the musician who left his country to find his song, but always kept Poland in his heart.

# TIMELINE

| | |
|---|---|
| **1810** | Frédéric François Chopin is born on March 1 in Zelazowa Wola, a village outside Warsaw. His family moves to Warsaw soon after. |
| **1816** | Chopin has his first piano lessons by the Czech teacher Wojciech Zywny. He practices pieces by Bach and Mozart. |
| **1817** | Chopin writes his first known pieces, two polonaises. |
| **1818** | Chopin's first concert in Warsaw is a success. |
| **1823** | After studying at home as a boy, Chopin starts school at the Warsaw Lyceum and studies Latin, Greek, and other subjects. He makes lifelong friends at school. |
| **1825** | He performs for the czar. Chopin's first official work, Rondo in C Minor, op. 1, is published. |
| **1826** | Chopin devotes himself to music at the Warsaw Conservatory. He studies composition with Josef Elsner. He composes and takes organ lessons. |
| **1828** | Chopin travels to Berlin and Prague, and begins composing études. |
| **1829** | After graduation, Chopin travels with friends to Vienna and performs concerts. His music is published in Vienna. |
| **1830** | Chopin performs his Concerto no. 1 in E Minor, op. 11, and Concerto no. 2 in F Minor, op. 21, in Warsaw. He leaves Warsaw to build his career in Europe. In |

*(continued on following page)*

*(continued from previous page)*

Paris, the French Revolution of 1830 installs King Louis Philippe and the July Monarchy.

**1831** In Vienna, Chopin learns of the Polish uprising against Russia. He writes études, scherzos, mazurkas, and nocturnes. The uprising fails while Chopin is in Stuttgart, Germany. Chopin travels to Paris. Polish refugees welcome him, and he begins teaching.

**1832** On February 26, Chopin performs his Paris debut. His career is launched in Paris.

**1835** Chopin meets his parents at a health spa in Carlsbad, Bohemia. On his way home, he stops in Dresden, where he becomes friends with Maria Wodzinska, the daughter of Polish friends.

**1836** Chopin is devastated when his plans to marry Maria are discouraged by her parents. Chopin meets George Sand. They become romantically involved two years later.

**1838** Chopin performs for King Louis Philippe and in smaller concerts at famous salons. In November, he travels to Majorca with Sand and her children to escape the Paris winter.

**1839** Chopin becomes very ill. In February, he and Sand return to France. Chopin finishes his Preludes, op. 28. He and Sand spend time in Nohant before going back to Paris.

| 1841 | After not performing in public for a long time, on April 26, Chopin gives a successful concert at the Salle Pleyel. |
| 1842 | Chopin moves to an elegant apartment in the Square d'Orleans. He writes his Ballade no. 4 in F Minor, op. 52. |
| 1844 | On May 3, Chopin's father, Mikolaj Chopin, dies. Chopin's health worsens, and his sister Ludwika arrives in France to be with him. |
| 1846 | Chopin spends his last summer with Sand in Nohant. |
| 1847 | Chopin and Sand part ways, and Chopin struggles with failing health. |
| 1848 | On February 16, Chopin performs his last concert in Paris. The Revolution of 1848 erupts on February 22. Chopin leaves Paris to stay in England and Scotland for seven months, where he teaches and performs. |
| 1849 | Back in Paris, Chopin is very sick. Ludwika comes from Warsaw to be by his side. He writes his last mazurka. On October 17, Chopin dies in Paris. His funeral is held at the Church of the Madeleine on October 30. He is buried in the Père Lachaise Cemetery in Paris. His heart is returned to a church in Warsaw. |

# LIST OF SELECTED WORKS

Piano Concerto no. 1 in E Minor, op. 11 (1830)

Piano Concerto no. 2 in F Minor, op. 21 (1830)

Nocturne no. 2 in E-flat Major, op. 9 (1830–1831)

Étude no. 12 in C Minor, op. 10 ("Revolutionary Étude") (1831)

Twelve Études, op. 10 (1829–1832)

Mazurka no. 4 in A Minor, op. 17 (1834)

Nocturne no. 1 in C-sharp Minor, op. 27 (1835)

Fantaisie-Impromptu in C-sharp Minor, op. 66 (1835) *(published posthumously)*

24 Preludes, op. 28 (1836–1839)

Piano Sonata no. 2 in B-flat Minor, op. 35 ("Funeral March" Sonata) (1839)

Nocturne No. 2 in F-sharp Minor, op. 48 (1841)

Ballade no 4 in F Minor, op. 52 (1842)

Polonaise in A-flat Major, op. 53 ("Heroic Polonaise") (1842)

Piano Sonata No. 3 in B Minor, op. 58 (1844)

Polonaise-Fantaisie in A-flat Major, op. 61 (1845–1846)

Waltz no. 1 in D-flat Major, op. 64 ("Minute Waltz") (1846–1847)

Seventeen Songs, op. 74 (1829–1847)

# GLOSSARY

**arpeggio** Sounding the notes of a chord one after another, instead of together.

**ballade** Long, dramatic piano work that is like a poem.

**counterpoint** The art of combining several musical lines at once, according to a system of rules.

**dissonance** Sounding together of notes with a roughness or tension.

**legato** Instruction to play a musical passage in a smooth, graceful style.

**movement** Self-contained section of a larger piece of music.

**nocturne** Quiet piece of music inspired by night.

**polonaise** Traditional, stately Polish court dance.

**prelude** Piece of music written to be played before other music; Chopin's twenty-four preludes are short piano pieces.

**scherzo** Italian word meaning "joke"; used for music that is lively, fast, and full of feeling.

**sonata** Musical composition for piano and other instruments with three or four movements, each having a different key, mood, and tempo.

**tempo** Instructions in a score defining speed and manner of performing music.

**tempo rubato** Italian phrase for speeding up or slowing down the tempo. Chopin changed the tempo of the right hand while that of the left hand remained constant.

# FOR MORE INFORMATION

Chopin Foundation of the United States
1440 79th Street Causeway, Suite 117
Miami, FL 33141
(305) 864-2349
Web site: http://www.ampolinstitute.org.ic.pl/_engine/
    page_render.asp

Cultural Services of the French Embassy
972 Fifth Avenue
New York, NY 10021
(212) 439-1407
Web site: http://www.frenchculture.org

The Frederick Chopin Society in Warsaw
Ostrogski Castle, Okólnik 1 Street
00-368 Warsaw
(48 22)827 54 71
Web site: http://www.chopin.pl

## WEB SITES

Due to the changing nature of Internet links, Rosen
Publishing has developed an online list of Web sites
related to the subject of this book. This site is updated
regularly. Please use this link to access the list:

http://www.rosenlinks.com/mth/chwo

# FOR FURTHER READING

Cavalletti, Carlo. *Chopin and Romantic Music* (Masters of Music). New York, NY: Barron's Educational Series, 2000.

Collins, David R. *Hero on Horseback: The Story of Casimir Pulaski*. New York, NY: Pelican Publishing Company, 1997.

Hovey, Tamara. *A Mind of Her Own: A Life of the Writer George Sand*. New York, NY: Harper & Row, 1977.

Hugo, Victor. *The Hunchback of Notre Dame*. New York, NY: Tor Books, 1996.

Krull, Kathleen. *Lives of the Musicians: Good Times, Bad Times* (And What the Neighbors Thought). San Diego, CA: Harcourt, 2002.

Liszt, Franz. *Life of Chopin*. Mineola, NY: Dover Publications, 2006.

Popescu, Julian. *Poland* (Major World Nations). Broomall, PA: Chelsea House, 2000.

Vernon, Roland. *Introducing Chopin* (Introducing Composers). Broomall, PA: Chelsea House, 2000.

Whiting, Jim. *The Life and Times of Frédéric Chopin* (Masters of Music: The World's Greatest Composers). Hockessin, DE: Mitchell Lane Publishers, 2005.

# BIBLIOGRAPHY

Chopin, Frédéric. *Chopin's Letters: Collected by Henry K. Opienski*. New York, NY: Dover Publications, 1988.

Doumic, Rene. *Biography of George Sand*. World Wide School. Retrieved January 7, 2007 (http://www. worldwideschool.org/library/books/hst/biography/ BiographyofGeorgeSand/chap2.html).

Eisler, Benita. *Chopin's Funeral*. New York, NY: Alfred A. Knopf, 2003.

Hovey, Tamara. *A Mind of Her Own: A Life of the Writer George Sand*. New York, NY: Harper & Row, 1977.

Huneker, James. *Chopin: The Man and His Music*. New York, NY: Dover, 1966.

Orga, Ates. *Chopin*. London, England: Omnibus Press, 1983.

Prideaux, Tom. *The World of Delacroix: 1798–1863*. New York, NY: Time-Life, 1966.

Rosen, Charles. *The Romantic Generation*. Cambridge, MA: Harvard University Press, 1995.

Samson, Jim. *Chopin*. New York, NY: Oxford University Press, 1996.

Sand, George. *Story of My Life*. New York, NY: SUNY Press, 1991.

Sand, George. *Winter in Majorca*. Chicago, IL: Academy Chicago Publishers, 1956.

Szulc, Tad. *Chopin in Paris*. New York, NY: Da Capo Press, 1998.

Weinstock, Herbert. *Chopin: The Man and His Music*. New York, NY: Knopf, 1969.

# INDEX

## ABOUT THE AUTHOR

While researching this book, author Ann Malaspina attended a concert of the Wroclaw Philharmonic, a Polish orchestra, at Lincoln Center. The young Polish pianist, Stanislaw Drzewiecki, performed Chopin's Concerto in E Minor. The audience included many Polish immigrants, and they applauded wildly at the finish. Chopin performed the same concerto on October 11, 1830, in Warsaw. He was just twenty years old, and it was his last performance before he left Poland forever. After hearing the concerto and watching the audience's emotional reaction, Malaspina began to understand the magic Chopin created with his music. She has been writing nonfiction for young people since 1997.

## PHOTO CREDITS

Cover, p. 48 akg-images; p. 4 The Art Archive/Society of The Friends of Music Vienna/Dagli Orti; p. 8 © Muzeum Narodowe, Warsaw, Poland/The Bridgeman Art Library; p. 12 The Art Archive/Chopin Birthplace Poland/Dagli Orti; p. 17 Archives Charmet, Bibliothèque des Arts Décoratifs, Paris, France/The Bridgeman Art Library; pp. 19, 30 © Henry Guttman/Getty Images; p. 25 University of Chicago Library, Special Collections Research Center; pp. 32, 42 © Lebrecht Music & Arts/The Image Works; p. 35 Erich Lessing/Art Resource, NY; p. 39 Réunion des Musées Nationaux/Art Resource, NY; p. 54 © Mansell/Time-Life Pictures/Getty Images.

**Designer:** Nelson Sá; **Photo Researcher:** Amy Feinberg

Gordon Gregory Middle School
2621 Springdale Circle
Naperville, IL 60564